1,000,000 Books

are available to read at

Forgotten Books

www.ForgottenBooks.com

Read online
Download PDF
Purchase in print

ISBN 978-0-243-53179-0
PIBN 10803308

This book is a reproduction of an important historical work. Forgotten Books uses state-of-the-art technology to digitally reconstruct the work, preserving the original format whilst repairing imperfections present in the aged copy. In rare cases, an imperfection in the original, such as a blemish or missing page, may be replicated in our edition. We do, however, repair the vast majority of imperfections successfully; any imperfections that remain are intentionally left to preserve the state of such historical works.

Forgotten Books is a registered trademark of FB &c Ltd.
Copyright © 2018 FB &c Ltd.
FB &c Ltd, Dalton House, 60 Windsor Avenue, London, SW19 2RR.
Company number 08720141. Registered in England and Wales.

For support please visit www.forgottenbooks.com

1 MONTH OF FREE READING

at
www.ForgottenBooks.com

By purchasing this book you are eligible for one month membership to ForgottenBooks.com, giving you unlimited access to our entire collection of over 1,000,000 titles via our web site and mobile apps.

To claim your free month visit:
www.forgottenbooks.com/free803308

* Offer is valid for 45 days from date of purchase. Terms and conditions apply.

English
Français
Deutsche
Italiano
Español
Português

www.forgottenbooks.com

Mythology Photography **Fiction** Fishing Christianity **Art** Cooking Essays Buddhism Freemasonry Medicine **Biology** Music **Ancient Egypt** Evolution Carpentry Physics Dance Geology **Mathematics** Fitness Shakespeare **Folklore** Yoga Marketing **Confidence** Immortality Biographies Poetry **Psychology** Witchcraft Electronics Chemistry History **Law** Accounting **Philosophy** Anthropology Alchemy Drama Quantum Mechanics Atheism Sexual Health **Ancient History** **Entrepreneurship** Languages Sport Paleontology Needlework Islam **Metaphysics** Investment Archaeology Parenting Statistics Criminology **Motivational**

EXTRACT *from letter of* Mr. EDWARD HERON-ALLEN, *translator of the prose version on which these quatrains are founded, to the Author.*

"You have achieved a task which I have always considered—and declared—to be impossible of accomplishment. I return your own list of revisions, having crossed out those which I do not consider to be improvements. Pray understand that my own notes on your manuscript are merely suggestions, and are not, in the vast majority of cases, to be regarded as necessary emendations.

"I shall look forward to the publication of your work with very great interest."

OF

OMAR KHAYYÁM

FROM A LITERAL PROSE TRANSLATION, BY EDWARD
HERON-ALLEN, OF THE EARLIEST KNOWN MANUSCRIPT
(Bodleian Library : Ouseley MSS., No. 140)

DONE INTO VERSE

BY

ARTHUR B. TALBOT

LONDON
ELKIN MATHEWS, VIGO STREET, W.
M CM IX

SECOND THOUSAND
CORRECTED AND REVISED

All rights reserved

TO

LOUIS PIERPOINT

IN GRATEFUL ACKNOWLEDGMENT OF MY FIRST

INTRODUCTION TO

OMAR KHAYYÁM

NOTE

THE history of Edward FitzGerald's *magnum opus*, the Ruba'iyát of Omar Khayyám, is too well known to need more than a brief recapitulation. The collection of quatrains—*ruba'iyát*—was first brought to his notice by Professor E. B. Cowell, lately Professor of Arabic and Sanskrit in the University of Cambridge, in the year 1855, when the earliest known manuscript of the *ruba'iyát* was discovered by the latter among the uncatalogued MSS. of the Ouseley Collection, in the Bodleian Library at Oxford. From a copy of this manuscript, made for him by Professor Cowell, FitzGerald translated, by means of a system of adaptation little short of marvellous, this early record of Antinomian Persian philosophy, or ethics, into English quatrains, of the same metric construction as the originals.

The same manuscript, which was solely responsible for the first edition of FitzGerald's work, was reproduced in photographic facsimile, and literally translated into English prose, by Mr. Edward Heron-Allen, in the year

1898, with a view to showing how far FitzGerald's work was a correct rendering of the original, and how far an adaptation.

It is now generally admitted that much of FitzGerald's beautiful poem was born of his own inventive genius, and is not to be found in the original. Nor does that admission detract from the merit of a work that has bestowed so many gems of thought and expression upon the English language, and earned for its author undying fame.

The Author of the present volume has cast Mr. Heron-Allen's literal prose translation into a metric form, also adhering to that of the original, and his aim has been to give as literal a rendering as possible. With what fidelity and what success that task has been accomplished, the Author must leave to the judgment of those readers whose interest in the matter may lead them to compare his work with the literal prose translation referred to.

The Author cannot close this brief note without thanking Mr. Heron-Allen for his great kindness in making many valuable suggestions, and in collating these quatrains with the original Persian.

A. B. T.

LEICESTER, *September*, 1908.

QUATRAINS

OF

OMAR KHAYYÁM

1

ALTHOUGH I have not serv'd Thee from my youth,
And though my face is mask'd with Sin uncouth,
In Thine Eternal Justice I confide,
As one who ever sought to follow Truth.

2

Perchance within the tavern I may see
The inmost secret of Thy Mystery,
While at the Shrine in ignorance I bow;
Burn me or bless me; I am part of Thee.

Blame not the Sinner; hast thou Innocence?
Lay thou aside imposture and pretence;
If thou would'st henceforth live a restful life
Give humble folk no reason for offence.

4

So rule thy life as ever to refrain
From strife that to thy fellow bringeth pain;
But scourge thyself, nor any mercy show,
If the Eternal Peace thou would'st attain.

5

O Queen of Night, for whom my spirit yearns,
Drink of the Wine of Life while yet Life burns!
How knowest thou that thou art not the one
To whom no moon or morrow e'er returns?

6

We dabble in the Qur'án now and then,
Read, and repent, yet fall from Grace again;
But in the goblet is engrav'd a text
That greets eternally the eyes of men.

7

We are! Here is the Wine! and here, close by,
The ruin'd furnace in a heap doth lie;
But when true inspiration we imbibe,
The very Elements we may defy.

8

'Twere better that thou makest but few friends;
Distance in intercourse to virtue tends;
Examine him in whom thy trust is placed,
He may be using thee for treach'rous ends.

9

This jug, o'er which I pledge my love to-day,
Was once a lover too, now sad, now gay;
The handle that thou seest upon its neck
Once round another's neck in friendship lay.

10

Ah! woeful is the heart from passion free,
And sweet the pain of lovers' misery!
If thou hast spent a day bereft of Love,
For evermore that day is lost to thee.

11

To-day with Youth's effulgency I shine,
And taste the Joy of Life in Youth's own Wine.
Sneer not because I find it bitter-sweet;
There lies its likeness to this life of mine.

12

To-morrow is beyond To-day's command,
And Sorrow lords it o'er the future land;
Thine hour is Now! Fix not thine eyes afar,
Missing the Glory ready to thy hand!

13

The world sighs out for Happiness, and saith
"The very desert liveth: where is Death?"
The hand of Moses blooms on many a bough,
And every breeze is sweet with Jesus' breath.

14

Truth's branches bear good fruit for all who seek;
They shake in vain who shake with hands too weak.
To-day resembles Yesterday, but lo!
Creation's voice shall in To-morrow speak.

15

This, in the Dawn ot Being, my behest,
My wand'ring soul for Heav'n and Hell made quest,
For Pen and Tablet; till the Teacher said
"Thou hast them all, O Man, within thy breast!"

16

But bring me Wine; for words I do not care;
I have thy lips, and all my Heav'n is there;
Bring wine to match thy cheeks; my penitence
Is full of tangles as thy clust'ring hair.

17

The breath of Spring is sweet unto the Rose,
The lov'd one's face in the dark garden grows;
Speak not of Yesterday,—I know it not,—
To-day is all thy wooing lover knows.

18

How long shall I throw pebbles on the sea?
What are the Idol-worshippers to me?
Who says "Khayyám is surely doomed to Hell?"
Hast thou been there? Hath Heaven rejected thee?

19

The Craftsman who hath made a cup so rare
To hold his wine, will handle it with care.
For love of whom, then, made He thee and me,
For hate of whom to break and not to spare?

20

Like Wind or Water, passing on its way,
Out of my life goes yet another day.
Two days there are that never trouble me—
One has not come, the other could not stay.

21

I was not asked to choose my natal morn,
I die as helplessly as I was born.
Bring wine, and I will strive to wash away
The recollection of Creation's scorn.

22

Khayyám, who stitch'd at Wisdom's golden tent,
Through Sorrow's white-hot furnaces was sent;
The tent-rope of his life by Fate was cut,
And for a song he from the Broker went.

23

Khayyám! for all thy sins pray do not deign
To mourn; thy grief can earn thee naught but pain.
Mercy was made for Sinners. Why then grieve?
For they who sin not, Mercy may not gain.

24

In cell and cloister, mosque and synagogue,
Are men whose steps the fear of Hell doth dog;
But he who carries God within his breast
Is independent of the Pedagogue.

25

If in the Spring, she whom I love so well
Meet me by some green bank—the truth I tell—
Bringing my thirsty soul a cup of wine,
I want no better Heaven, nor fear a Hell.

26

Know this, that soon thou diest, and thy soul
The Book of God's Great Secret must unroll;
Be happy! knowing not whence thou hast come,
Nor whither thou shalt go. Drink out the Bowl!

27

Falling asleep, I heard my Fate confess
That Sleep ne'er bore the Rose of Happiness.
" Sleep is the Mate of Death," she cried.   " Awake !
Drink, ere Her lips bestow the last caress ! "

28

Then inspiration from on High I sought,
Asking that Knowledge might to me be brought;
But presently my heart said, " Pray no more !
The power of Prayer is all, the Prayer is naught ! "

29

Behind a veil the Gods their Secrets keep,
And past that curtain none may hope to peep;
One plot of earth is all we may secure.
Drink, then ! for such philosophies are cheap.

30

The Gods in mortal man do not confide,
And Fate from fools her mysteries doth hide;
Be thou but just towards thy fellow man,
All hope or fear thou mayest put aside.

31

For He, to whom all future things are known,
E'en as He made thee wrote thy record down;
And what His pen hath written, good or ill,
No strife may alter, and no grief atone.

32

If thou could'st sit beside a rippling stream,
With her of all thy thoughts the constant theme,
Quaffing the Sunshine and the Wine of Morn,
No call to prayer, methinks, would break thy dream.

33

Tired am I. The Firmament my belt;
A mighty river are the tears I've spilt;
Hell is a spark struck by my restless soul,
And Heaven the joy my tranquil heart hath felt.

34

Men talk of Eden's Houris and their charms;
To maids of Earth I drink and sing my psalms.
Hold fast Life's cash; if Time be in thy debt
How pleasant is the distant call to arms!

35

Drink Wine: for 'neath the clay in silent gloom
Long shalt thou sleep, with none to share thy tomb;
Reveal this hidden secret unto none—
The wither'd tulip ne'er again will bloom.

36

Drink Wine: for here, and now, Eternal Life
Gives all the gain that Youth may win from Strife;
Roses and friends to share thy merriment:
Seize now that Joy with which to-day is rife!

37

Give me red wine my broken heart to heal,
Wine, the good friend of all that passion feel;
I find more comfort in a single draught
Than hollow Heaven bestows on those who kneel.

38

I drink, and spiteful folk attempt to show
That Virtue no worse enemy could know;
But if Religion stands in fear of wine,
Then let me quaff the blood of such a foe!

39

Wine is a melted ruby, and the cup
The mine from which we mortals dig it up;
The cup the body, and the wine the soul:
How many tears lie hidden where we sup?

40

Whether my destin'd fate shall be to dwell
Midst Heaven's joys or in the fires of Hell
I know not; here with Spring, and bread, and wine,
And thee, my love, my heart says " All is well."

41

The joy or pain that Fate's decrees allow,
The good or ill inscribed upon Man's brow;
Impute them not unto the Heavens above,
For Heaven is ruled by Fate as much as thou

42

If in thy heart the seed of Love is plac'd,
No day of all thy life can run to waste;
Whether for God's approval thou dost strive,
Or on the joys of Earth hast set thy taste.

43

Where'er the Rose or Tulip scents the air,
The life-blood of a King has ebb'd forth there;
And every Violet that decks the Earth
Was once a mole upon a cheek so fair.

44

Be wise: thou canst not see what Fate portends;
Be arm'd against the sharpened sword she sends;
Feast not upon the sweets she offers thee,
For poison with the sugar oft she blends.

45

My empty purse on wine must cast the blame:
My kisses, love, have robbed thee of thy fame;
Some pledge themselves to faith in Heav'n or Hell:
But who hath been to Hell? From Heav'n who came?

46

O thou, whose cheek is modell'd like the Rose,
No brighter eye far Cathay's idol shows;
Thy glance hath taught the Shah of Babylon
Each move that Life's eventful chessboard knows.

47

Who cares for Balkh or Baghdad? Life is fleet;
And what though bitter be the cup, or sweet,
So it be full? This Moon, when we are gone,
The circling months will day by day repeat.

48

For, those who from the date its vintage take,
And they who áll night long devotions make,
All are submerg'd, not one remains on Earth,
All are asleep: One only is awake.

49

The Voice that haunts thy peace, within thy brain
A hundred times a day sings this refrain :—
" Thou livest but a moment, and art not
Like herbs which, gathered once, spring up again."

50

The Slaves of Intellect in talk persist;
Die, arguing does this or that exist;
Fools eat dry raisins till their souls become
Sour grapes; but wise men on New Wine insist.

51

The Universe gained nothing from my birth,
Nor will my going cause it any dearth
Of dignity or beauty.   None can say
Why I should come to, or why leave, the Earth.

52

To Love's effacement this our life we trust,
And into Fate's strong talons we are thrust;
Then rouse thyself, O sweet-faced Cupbearer,
Bring me a draught, for long shall I be dust!

53

Our happiness is but an empty sign :
One old and faithful friend we have—New Wine;
Stretch out the merry hand unto the cup,
'Tis all the Good within thy reach or mine!

54

Whate'er the Pen hath written stands for aye :
Affliction's sword the grieving heart will slay ;
Though all thy life with anguish thou art wrung,
The forward march of Fate thou canst not stay.

55

O Heart ! Seek not the frail ones for awhile,
And cease with Love existence to beguile !
Frequent the house of them that beg and pray,
Perchance on thee such holy ones may smile.

56

The stars that yon great firmament adorn
Have birth and death, and yet again are born
And in the skirt of Heaven, the womb of Earth,
Are they whom God will yet bring to the morn.

57

The hypocrites who make Belief a law,
'Twixt Soul and Body nice distinctions draw;
But I would still maintain my faith in Wine,
Though in the goblet Death himself I saw.

58

The circling planets, that in space abound,
The brains of our most learnèd ones confound;
Hold fast the Cord, for they that make thee spin,
Themselves with giddiness will turn around!

59

I do not dread Extinction : far more bliss
Lies in that half of Time than lives in this;
This life was lent by God, and unto Him
I will surrender what I shall not miss.

60

Life's caravan mysteriously goes by ;
Seize Happiness, while yet the moments fly !
Do not, Cupbearer, for to-morrow grieve,
Bring Wine to-night, e'er Dawn lights up the sky !

61

Though old, with love for thee I am forlorn,
Or else the wine thou bringest I would scorn ;
Thou hast destroy'd my early penitence :
The garment Patience sewed the Years have torn.

62

My veil of Temperance by wine is rent,
But still with wine my soul shall be content ;
How can the vintners purchase better goods
Than those which to the market they have sent ?

63

Why wert Thou once so loving, and didst try
My soul, with softest blandishments, to buy?
To-day Thou sendest naught but dismal woe;
How have I sinn'd? Once more I ask Thee, why?

64

My soul to Love for ever I commit:
My body from the Grape shall never flit;
They say, "May God repentance give thee soon;"
He gives it not, so I will none of it.

65

Ablution in the tavern needs much wine;
The tarnish'd reputation ne'er will shine;
Be happy! for our veil of Temperance
Is torn beyond repair. Why then repine?

66

I saw, upon the terrace, one who trod
In blind contempt upon the beaten sod.
The bruisèd clay in mystic language spake—
"Thou, too, shalt some day feel the Foot of God!'

67

The day is fair, and free from cold or heat,
And rain hath wash'd the dust from roses sweet;
The nightingale cries in the Ancient Tongue—
"Drink, pallid rose, and blush at Love's pulse-beat!"

68

E'er thou art stricken down by Fate above,
Drink wine, the rosy wine that speaks of Love!
Thy body hath no value; from the grave
No man will dig thee up for treasure trove!

69

With wine my bodily defects make good:
Tincture my amber visage with its blood;
With rosy wine my last ablutions make,
And build my coffin of the Vine's sweet wood.

70

O Shah! thy brows were crown'd by Destiny,
That saddl'd thine imperial steed for thee;
And where thy charger plants his golden hoof
Thine abject slaves a gilded footprint see.

71

Imaginary Love, a vain conceit,
Like to a fire half-dead, gives little heat.
A lover true with constant fervour burns,
To him nor peace, nor food, nor sleep, is sweet.

72

The tangled secrets of Eternity
Remain unsolv'd; and Time and Space are free
From Man's control; both ignorant and wise
Stand impotent before Infinity.

73

Restrain thy worldly tastes, and live content,
Careless alike of Good and Evil sent;
Take wine and kisses, ere it be too late,
For few such days remain to thee unspent.

74

The Heavens rain down their benefits divine,
Their blossom-gifts in every garden shine;
I pour red wine into this lily-cup,
As purple clouds pour down sweet jessamine.

75

For wine, good men athirst will always pant
But to such trifles God no thought will grant;
He knew, before He made me, I should drink:
And, if I drink not, was He ignorant?

76

Let not the Veil of Sorrow shroud thy face,
Nor in thy life let idle grief find place;
But feast on books, and love, and Nature's joys,
Ere Earth enfold thee in her last embrace.

77

Drink Wine, that heals all woes, and thou shalt yet
The seventy-two contentious sects forget;
Shun not that Alchemist, who in the Cup
A draught to cure a thousand ills hath set.

78

Is Wine an evil? Tell me first who drinks,
How much he thirsts, with whom his glass he clinks?
If these conditions three be meetly fill'd,
No son of Wisdom from the grape-juice shrinks.

79

Drink Wine, for thou shalt be resolv'd in Earth,
And, as a goblet, shalt find second birth;
Heedless be thou of Heav'n and Hell alike;
Be not deceiv'd! Hold fast to Wine and Mirth!

80

The sweet Spring-breezes now the world adorn,
In hope of rain its eyes salute the morn;
The hands of Moses whiten many a spray,
The breath of Jesus moves the thrusting corn.

81

Lo! every drop the cupbearer shall spill,
The fire of anguish in some eye may still;
Praise be to God! Thou knowest that in Wine
Is that which frees thy heart from every ill.

82

Each morn the dew begems the tulip's face,
The violet's bended crest is full of grace;
But, fairest of them all, the rosebud sweet,
With modest blush her skirt doth closely lace.

83

Friends, when ye meet together, ne'er forget
The one, whom o'er the cup ye oft have met;
And, when ye drink a draught of wholesome wine,
At my turn, upside down a goblet set!

84

Friends, when ye keep a tryst, and meet your host,
And merrymake with those ye love the most,
When the Mugh Wine the cupbearer takes round,
Drink to a certain Helpless One a toast!

85

One draught outweighs a hundred hearts and creeds,
And he who drinks no Eastern Empire needs;
Save ruby wine, there is not on the Earth
One bitter thing that so much sweetness breeds.

86

If thou desirest Him, put all from thee:
No earthly love must in thy bosom be;
Whatever is, will hinder thine advance:
How canst thou fare thus burden'd? Be thou free!

87

Bring me that Ruby in its crystal mine:
Bring me the friend that good men call divine.
Thou knowest that this temporary world
Is but a passing zephyr.   Bring me Wine!

88

Bring physic to this heart with sorrow drear,
Bring wine, musk-scented, rosy-tinted, clear.
Dost thou not know of Sorrow's antidote?—
Wine to thy lips, and Music to thine ear.

89

In the Bazaar I saw, but yesterday,
A potter rudely pounding the fresh clay;
The clay in mystic language made complaint—
"I too was once like thee: thy hand then stay!"

90

Drink of that Wine which is Eternal Life!
With its Sunshine the joys of youth are rife:
Like fire it burns, but ah! what happiness
It bears to hearts that break in Sorrow's strife!

91

Scout the Traditions: bid the Law begone:
The morsel that thou hast withhold from none:
By word nor deed afflict a single heart:
I'll guarantee thee future worlds.   Drink on!

92

Wine is rose-red, perchance the Rose's tears
Lie in the cup, or it a ruby bears:
A ruby melted in her essence sweet,
As moonlight melting when the Sun appears.

93

We break each vow: upon ourselves once more
Of fame and fair repute we shut the door;
Reproach me not with folly, for, in truth,
The Wine of Love hath caught me, as of yore.

94

To speak plain language, parable to shame,
We are the pieces, Heaven plays the game:
A childish game upon the board of Life,
Then back into the Box from whence we came.

95

O heart! truth absolute thou canst not see,
Then why abase thyself in misery?
Bow down to Fate, and wrestle not with Time!
The Pen will not rewrite one word for thee.

96

But still the Rose's face the shadows fret,
Still doth my heart the wine-desire beget;
Sleep not, my love, it is not time to sleep,
But bring me wine, for daylight lingers yet!

97

Fling dust at Heaven, that every offering spurns;
Drink wine, and love while thy desire yet burns;
What time is this to worship or to pray?
Of all that have departed, none returns.

98

Fill up the cup! the day breaks white like snow;
Learn colour from the Wine's deep ruby glow;
Two fragrant aloe-logs will cheer us all;
Make this a lute, that on the embers throw.

99

Our old debauch we come now to revive,
Again we have renounc'd the Pray'r-times five;
Where'er the goblet is, there shall we be,
Our necks extended, each a flask alive.

100

To the jar's mouth my eager lip I press'd,
For Life's Elixir making anxious quest;
It join'd its lip to mine, and whisper'd low—
" Drink wine : thou shalt not wake from thy last rest ! "

101

Here is good counsel, give thine ear to me,
Wear not the garment of hypocrisy;
The Future is unending, Life is short,
Sell not for it the whole Eternity.

102

Khayyám, though drunk, lift up thy cheerful voice,
Be happy with the darling of thy choice;
If in the end of things thou must be naught,
Imagine thou art nothing now. Rejoice!

103

Within a potter's shop, ere this day broke,
I saw a host of pots—some mute, some spoke;
And suddenly one pot, aggressive, cried,
" Who makes, or buys, or sells, us earthen folk ? "

104

Of this good spirit, that men call Pure Wine,
They say, " Twill heal that broken heart of thine."
Haste then, and bring me three o'erbrimming cups,
Impute no evil to a gift divine.

105

Regard my virtues singly, bid them live,
But pass my crimes, by tens, through Memory's sieve;
Bear not resentment, God must be the judge;
By great Muhammad's Tomb, I say, " Forgive ! "

106

Wine in the goblet is a spirit rare,
Within the jar a tender soul is there;
No earthly thing may be the friend of wine
Except the cup, which, though of clay, is fair.

107

Where doth the past begin, the future end?
Rejoice to-day, Wine is thy only friend!
Nor theory nor practice is of use,
But Wine unties each knot that Fate may send.

108

This vault of Heaven, 'neath which like fools we sit,
Is but a magic-lantern, dimly lit:
The Sun the flame, the Universe the lamp,
We are the figures that revolve in it.

109

I do not always o'er the flesh prevail,
I suffer for the sin: must I bewail?
Upon Thy generous pardon I rely,
Because I grieve that Thou should'st see me frail.

110

Let me arise, and in pure wine drink deep,
And bid my cheeks their ripe-fruit colour keep
Then will I throw in meddling Reason's face
Sufficient wine to make her fall asleep.

111

How long shall we be slaves, untying knots?
Who cares if Fate long life, or short, allots?
Pour out a cup of wine, before we all
Become, within the workshop, earthen pots.

112

Since our abode in this world is so short,
Sans Wine and Love this Life were sorry sport.
Creeds, old or new, how long will ye discuss?
Shall I, when dead, bestow on Time a thought?

113

A hundred sins there are in loving Thee,
Loving Thee not incurs grave penalty.
If I keep lifelong faith unto Thy scourge,
Give me the credit when Thou judgest me!

114

I am all artifice. Since Time is swift,
In joy and wine I see no need for thrift;
They say, " May God to thee grant penitence."
He gives it not, nor would I take the gift.

115

Though to the Mosque I come with pious air,
By Allah! think not I have come for prayer;
I stole a mat once from a worshipper—
That sin worn out, again I here repair.

116

When Fate hath trampl'd me beneath her feet,
And torn me from the hope of Life so sweet,
Make nothing but a goblet of my clay;
When full of wine my heart once more may beat.

117

I know not which the bait, or which the snare
'Twixt Mosque and Cup I'm drawn, now here, now there;
And yet the Cup, my Darling One, and I,
Are better ripe in wine, than green in prayer.

118

'Tis morn ! The breath of wine let us inhale;
Break on a stone this cup of honour frail !
Let us cease striving for our Ancient Hope,
That lute and love may yet our hearts regale.

119

We chose dry bread and privacy, before
The luxury that wealth may have in store.
We have bought poverty with heart and soul,
And poverty hath but enrich'd us more.

120

I know, though outwardly, of Life and Death;
And, inwardly, of all above, beneath;
But let me boast not, for I nothing know
Beyond the inspiration of Wine's breath.

121

A teacher once we sought, when young, to find
Wisdom that for a while contents the mind;
And from the whole discourse what did we learn?—
We come like water and depart like wind.

122

To him who understands Life's mystery,
Its joy or sorrow all the same must be;
Since good and ill alike must end, who cares
Whether it be all pain or remedy?

123

So far as in thee lies, feast evermore,
And cast both prayer and fasting from thy door.
From Omar Khayyám hear the word of truth,—
" Rob on the road, and drink—but feed the poor.

124

This world one choice alone for men hath blest,
'Tis either Death, or Life by pain opprest;
How happy he to whom Death quickly comes,
And he who ne'er is born hath perfect rest.

125

O Dervish! rend thy figur'd veil apart,
Rather than sacrifice to it thy heart!
Take on thy back the rug of poverty,—
A Sultan's equal 'neath that rug thou art!

126

Behold the evils Heav'n doth here display,
The world bereft of friends that pass away;
Gain for thyself a moment's happiness,
Nor Past nor Future seek,—behold To-day!

127

'Tis better here with Love and Wine to sit
Than to become the zealous hypocrite;
If all who love or drink are doom'd to Hell,
On whom shall Heaven bestow a benefit?

128

No happy heart with sorrow should consume,
No joyful life mid test and trial fume;
None can foretell the future; wine, and love,
And rest we need, so these let us resume.

129

The Heavens, that they may destroy us both,
On our pure souls to war are nothing loth;
Sit down, my Idol, on the grass, for soon
My dust and thine shall aid its vernal growth.

130

What profits it our birth, and what our death?
Where is the Woof our life's frail Warp beneath?
The World's great fire burns many such to dust;
Where is the smoke of them within its breath?

131

Flee from all study, and thy fingers twine
In those soft curls of her thou callest thine;
Ere Fate shall spill thy blood, hasten to pour
Into the cup the red blood of the vine.

132

This beard of mine hath brush'd the Tavern door.
The good and ill of Earth or Heav'n no more
I seek; though both the worlds should fall,
Here, like a drunkard, will I lie and snore.

133

To everything save wine deny thy lips;
And wine is best when Beauty pours and sips;
Drinking, and Beggary, and Sin are best;
From Pole to Pole all pleasures these eclipse.

134

This heavenly vault is like a fallen bowl,
'Neath which the captive wise in sorrow roll;
Revenge thyself! as do the cup and jar,
When wine is spilt between them cheek by jowl.

135

The Rose's skirt is tatter'd by the breeze,
But Nightingales still woo her in the trees;
Sit in her fragrant bower, for oft the wind
Hath strewn and turn'd to dust such flowers as these.

136

How long shall I, or poor or wealthy, grieve?
How long, or sad or merry, shall I live?
Fill up the bowl! this very breath I draw,
The winds may ne'er from me again receive.

137

Bear not the sorrow of this world of strife!
Wake not remembrance, for with Death 'tis rife!
Love her of fairy birth and glowing breast!
Drown not in water all the joys of Life!

138

Though sixty years thou countest, scorn to die;
Where'er thou walkest, to the wine-flask hie;
Until thy hollow skull be made a bowl,
Hold fast the jar, nor let the cup go by.

139

Old wine is better than a kingdom new;
Walk not, save towards the wine of rosy hue.
The cup is worth a hundred Persian thrones,
Its cover worth the crown of Kai-Khosrú.

140

O Sákí! they whose souls from them have fled,
In self-content have bow'd their sleepy head;
Go thou and drink, but hear the truth from me,
For 'tis but wind, whatever they have said.

141

My wine, O Lord, Thou spillest on the sward,
On me the door of happiness hast barr'd;
Thy Hand hath broken my poor jug of wine,
But, by my life, Thy ways are strange, O Lord!

142

To each base creature, something Thou hast given;
By Thy cool streams the face of earth is riven;
The pure man, for a crust, will stake his all:
Thou should'st give readily, for such, a Heaven.

143

O Heart! the Fount of Truth thou dost not gain,
To thee Philosophy makes nothing plain;
Build thyself here a Heaven with wine and cup,
For thou may'st ne'er another Heaven attain.

144

Creation's smoke seems evermore thy meat,
How long with sophistry thyself wilt cheat?
Thou want'st no stock-in-trade to waste away,
Nor capital.   All profits thou dost eat.

145

O Soul! if thou this dust aside canst fling,
And soar through space upon unfetter'd wing,
Infinity thy sphere—count it thy shame
That to this earth contented thou dost cling.

146

Last night I smote the winecup on a stone;
For such mad folly how may I atone?
The shatter'd cup, in mystic language, said,
" I was like thee, my fate shall be thine own."

147

O Heart's Desire! from cup and flask seek aid :
Be merry midst the river's flowery glade ;
Malicious Heav'n of many joyous folk
A hundred times hath cups and flagons made.

148

In every step I take Thou sett'st a snare,
Saying, " Thus will I entrap thee, so beware !"
And, while all things are under Thy command,
That I a rebel am Thou dost declare.

149

Give me a scroll of verse, a little wine,
With half a loaf to fill thy needs and mine,
And with the desert sand our resting place,
For ne'er a Sultan's kingdom would we pine.

150

Live happily, place not in grief thy trust,
Amidst injustice show that thou art just;
If all the world must come to nothingness,
Be free, and deem thyself already dust.

151

Where'er on earth my wand'ring gaze I place,
A garden lav'd by Kausar's stream I trace;
Heaven in the desert, Hell hath disappear'd,
And Paradise is in her Angel face.

152

Be happy! yesterday thy joy or pain
Was fix'd, and yesterday may none regain;
Live happy! for yestr'een, unsought, the Fates
What thou wilt do to-morrow did ordain.

153

Pour out this pure red wine of tulip hue,
And with the jar's clear blood the cup imbue.
Beside the wine-cup, there is not to-day
One friend of mine with heart so warm and true.

154

Heaven in my ear this secret did confess,
"From me all Fate's decrees thou may'st possess."
Were mine the hand that made myself revolve,
I would have sav'd myself much giddiness.

155

Let Fortune but provide me bread of wheat,
A gourd of wine, a bone of mutton sweet,
Then in the desert if we twain might sit,
Joys such as ours no Sultan could defeat.

156

Whene'er thy hand may reach two cups of wine,
Let wine's own light in each assembly shine;
For He who made the world cares less than naught
For thy moustaches, or for beards like mine.

157

Had I the power, I ne'er had borne Life's thrall,
Nor willingly would lie beneath the Pall.
Far better, were it not? if in this world
I ne'er had come, or gone, or liv'd at all.

158

Ramazán's end draws near, Shawwál doth break,
The time with flowers and joy to merry-make;
Now porters with their loads stand back to back
Laden with wine.—Up, bottles, and awake!

"THE REAL OMAR"

QUATRAINS OF OMAR KHAYYÁM

From a literal prose translation, by EDWARD HERON-ALLEN, *of the earliest known Manuscript (Bodleian Library: Ouseley MSS., No.* 140), *done into verse*

BY

ARTHUR B. TALBOT

Second Thousand, Corrected and Revised.
Cloth, 1*s.* 6*d.* net.   Paper, 1*s.* net.

EXTRACTS

FROM A COLUMN AND A HALF REVIEW OF THE ABOVE WORK (THEREIN REFERRED TO AS "THE REAL OMAR" IN

"*The Times*" *Literary Supplement* (29th October, 1908)

"He has set about producing a literal rendering in verse, based upon Mr. Heron-Allen's literal rendering in prose, and he has produced a translation, not only remarkable for fidelity, but of genuine poetical value.   One has only to turn a page or

EXTRACTS *from* "*The Times*" *Literary Supplement*—continued

two to acknowledge one merit with gratitude, for it is one which few of the quatrain-spinners share—he is wholly bent on rendering Omar for Omar's sake, and never makes him a vehicle for his own moods and conceits. Here is a stanza in Mr. Heron-Allen's prose and in Mr. Talbot's verse :—

> Of those who draw the pure date wine
> and those who spend the night in prayer,
> not one is on the dry land, all are in the water—
> One is awake; the others are asleep.

> For those who from the date its vintage take,
> And they who all night long devotions make,
> All are submerg'd, not one remains on Earth,
> All are asleep; One only is awake.

There can be no question of the fidelity of the translation of that stanza, and yet it has, particularly in the last line, the heightened meaning, the telling quality of genuine verse. Mr. Talbot, then, has one characteristic which inspires confidence from the first; and one's confidence is enhanced by the discovery of how resolutely he has also set himself against FitzGerald's mesmerism in keeping to the spirit as well as the letter of the text."

* * * * * *

"Mr. Talbot has taken it simply as it came. His version opens, therefore, not with FitzGerald's magnificent *réveillé*, but in the deepest and most contrite mood which Omar attains :—

EXTRACTS *from* "*The Times*" *Literary Supplement*—continued

> Although I have not served Thee from my youth,
> And though my face is mask'd with Sin uncouth,
> In Thine Eternal Justice I confide,
> As one who ever sought to follow Truth.
>
> Perchance within the tavern I may see
> The inmost secret of Thy Mystery,
> While at the Shrine in ignorance I bow;
> Burn me or bless me; I am part of Thee.

These two opening verses in Mr. Talbot's version are, in point of fact, nearer paraphrase and further from literal translation than the greater part of his work; but they have just the strength and sincerity which seem to inspire the original, and they give the key to that side of Omar which FitzGerald most ignored, but which Mr. Talbot has rendered best."

* * * * * *

"It is curious, indeed, that through all the sudden changes of mood and manner which characterize the original the leading trait of the poet's mind is a certain sad lucidity, which never really deserts him, however much he may pretend to fuddle his wits with wine; and this quality is more impressive in the desultory arrangement of stanzas in the text, faithfully reproduced by Mr. Talbot, though of necessity ignored in our quotations, than in the cumulative eloquence of FitzGerald's argument."

* * * * * *

Extracts *from* " *The Times* " *Literary Supplement*—continued

"That is, no doubt, no more than to say that, very wisely, he resists all temptations to draw the bow of Odysseus; but a result is that the general character of his verse is more faithful than FitzGerald's to the character of the original.

"Mr. Talbot does, however, in his own way often produce stanzas which one would find beautiful and wish to remember, even if one met them unattended, so to speak, and without references :—

> If thou could'st sit beside a rippling stream,
> With her of all thy thoughts the constant theme,
> Quaffing the Sunshine and the Wine of Morn,
> No call to prayer, methinks, would break thy dream.
>
> Give me a scroll of verse, a little wine,
> With half a loaf to fill thy needs and mine,
> And with the desert sand our resting-place,
> For ne'er a Sultan's kingdom would we pine.

It is something to have written that last stanza afresh after FitzGerald, and to have not absolutely failed. Mr. Talbot has, in fact, achieved a version of undoubted value to those who wish to know more of the real Omar and cannot read him in his own tongue."

LONDON : ELKIN MATHEWS, VIGO STREET, W.

QUATRAINS FROM OMAR KHAYYÁM

DONE INTO ENGLISH BY

F. YORK POWELL, M.A.

Regius Professor of Modern History in the University of Oxford, 1894-1904

Printed on hand-made paper at the Chiswick Press.

Pott 4to.   3*s*. net.

"This year (1901) York Powell printed the quintessence of his wisdom of Life, his confession of faith, his religion in his NOTE ON OMAR. . . . Indeed, he put a piece of his soul into the little preface. The stanzas, which are all in FitzGerald's measure, might have been from the hand of the founder. But the new thing is Powell's NOTE."—

See "Frederick York Powell: a Life," by Professor Oliver Elton, 8vo., Oxford, 1906. Vol. I.

LONDON: ELKIN MATHEWS, VIGO STREET, W.

"A WANDERING MINSTREL"
THE SONGS OF SIDI HAMMO

RENDERED INTO ENGLISH FOR THE FIRST TIME BY

R. L. N. JOHNSTON

Edited with a Preface by S. L. Bensusan, M.R.A.S., Author of "Morocco," with Facsimile and Cover-design. Royal 16mo. 2s. 6d. net.

"Mr. Johnston has done his work well, and the result is a really interesting addition to the store of North African folk-lore."—*Athenæum*.

"One of the most delightful little treasuries of a rare kind of folk-lore which you shall find in a day's march."—*Evening Standard*.

"This little volume, with its mystical cover, might easily pass unnoticed. Yet it is a gem of the first water. It contains the poetry of the chief minstrel of a people we know almost nothing about, whether in literature or history, and it is the first specimen of that poetry to appear in English.... No lover of poetry will disdain these pages of pure essence, the very altar of Berber love songs."—*Manchester Guardian*.

"One of the most curious and delightful feasts which a translator has given us for a very long time."—*Bookman*.

LONDON: ELKIN MATHEWS, VIGO STREET, W.

LONDON: PRINTED BY WILLIAM CLOWES AND SONS, LIMITED.

SD - #0123 - 281024 - C0 - 229/152/4 - PB - 9780243531790 - Gloss Lamination